HERITAGE TRACTION IN

Volume Three
THE DELTICS

NOSTALGIA ROAD PUBLICATIONS

The **Heritage Traction** Series ™

is produced under licence by
Nostalgia Road Publications Ltd.
Units 5 - 8, Chancel Place, Shap Road Industrial Estate,
Kendal, Cumbria, LA9 6NZ
Tel. +44 (0)1539 738832 - Fax: +44 (0)1539 730075

designed and published by
Trans-Pennine Publishing Ltd.
PO Box 10, Appleby-in-Westmorland, Cumbria, CA16 6FA
Tel. +44 (0)17683 51053 Fax. +44 (0)17683 53558
e-mail: admin@transpenninepublishing.co.uk

and printed by
Kent Valley Colour Printers Ltd.
Kendal, Cumbria - +44 (0)1539 741344

Front Cover: *With its classic twin exhaust plumes we are again reminded of the early prototype's days at Liverpool Lime Street. However, by 23rd November 1980 the final weeks in traffic are fast approaching for the class as a whole and for 55015* Tulyar *in particular.* Matthew Hall (D1100)

Rear Cover Top: *The nameboards on 55009* Alycidon *say it all, in a melancholy scene at the Doncaster Works on 'Deltic Open Day' 27th February 1982.* Steve Ireland (D1101)

Rear Cover Bottom: *Pictured on that same great 'Deltic Open Day' when all the remaining class members were assembled for the enthusiasts at Doncaster, we find 55007* Pinza. *Matthew Hall (D1102)

Title Page: *Whilst working the 'Flying Scotsman' service, with the brand new XP64 rake of coaches trailing behind, D9014* The Duke of Wellington's Regiment, *is viewed in August 1964 on the through road at Selby.* Richard Sinclair Collection (D1103)

This Page: *This may act as a reminder to those who were at Doncaster on 27th February 1982 for that Deltic requiem, which shows how BR expected their visitors to enjoy themselves!* Steve Ireland Collection (D1199)

INTRODUCTION

In 1955 the English Electric Company built a prototype diesel-electric locomotive as a private venture at its Vulcan Works, Newton-Le-Willows. The prototype, named *Deltic*, after its Delta-shaped engine design, was then tested on both the London Midland and Eastern regions during the 1950s, with the Eastern Region later placing an order for further locomotives in an attempt to retain some East Coast Main Line prestige over the West Coast route. With this order for 22 production models, English Electric's gamble paid off. The London Midland Region had however, made the decision to budget for the progressive electrification of their route north from Euston.

The East Coast Main Line would not be electrified for many years ahead, so the British Transport Commission were coaxed into an order for the supply of new 'Deltics' as the class inevitably became colloquially known, even though the extra cost for these Type 5 machines would be quite considerable.

Above: *Although it was not the first of the production Deltics, D9001* St. Paddy *was in fact the first to enter service. It is seen on 21st May 1967, having been the first in this row of locomotives to gain a full yellow nose panel. The distinctive sand filler gantry, clearly identifies the shed's location as Doncaster (36A).* Frank Hornby (D1105)

Contrast the published costs of an English Electric Type 1 (at £70,000 each) or a Type 4 (at £110,000 each) with the twin-engined Deltics, which were nearly £200,000 apiece. The production Deltics would therefore become the most expensive single unit diesel of their day, but they would also be the most powerful too. The unique twin 18-cylinder Napier engines would give a combined output of 3,300hp compared with the English Type 4 design's (post-TOPS Class 40) single 16-cylinder engine developing 2,000hp. The locomotive engines were based upon Napier's novel design high-speed marine units that were laid out in a triangular or Delta shape, and connected to DC dynamos in each case.

In order to base the 'test' locomotive close to the engine manufacturer's works (at Netherton near Liverpool), the trials were initially held along the West Coast Main Line. The prototype was used on the expresses between Liverpool and London, managing a healthy average of 650 to 700 miles per day, often showing the full potential of the power and acceleration that were possible from this design. This was no doubt noticed and appreciated by the men of the LMR who might just have been swayed into buying Deltics as replacements for their beloved 'Duchesses', rather than go for electrification.

One special trial involved BR Testing Staff on the famous Settle & Carlisle section of the LMR. With a 20-coach load of 642 tons, the Deltic set off on the 82$1/2$ miles from Carlisle to Hellifield, including the long drag to Ais Gill summit, 1,167 feet up into the Pennines.

Beyond Appleby this route runs upwards for 17 miles without a break, and almost all of it on a continuous 1:100 gradient. With its impressive load, the Deltic began this gruelling climb at 72mph but was still managing to do a respectable 47mph by the summit at Ais Gill. So it took just over 56 minutes for the 48 miles, from the start to the summit. Its average speed for the round trip was 56.2mph and this included the arduous ascents of Ais Gill from both directions.

This was without any excessive speeds or a loss of safety on the descents, and a fuel consumption that would indicate the locomotive could keep up this load at maximum effort for over six hundred miles, well beyond what would be asked of them in daily service. With these impressive operating figures, arguably the purchase price was not too bad after all.

However, the LMR was not to be diverted from its course of main line electrification, and as far as diesel traction was concerned it went for batches of BR-built 1Co-Co1 Type 4s (Peaks), along with the similar English Electric Type 4 D200 series, later Class 40.

Below: *Having been repainted blue and given the later style numerals, 9001 St. Paddy heads an Anglo-Scottish express into Doncaster in December 1973. When new on 11th January 1961 this locomotive was exhibited in an un-named condition at Stratford (30A), before being returned to Doncaster. It was taken into stock formally on 23rd February 1961, five days before going to Finsbury Park (34G). In the best Eastern Region traditions it was named at Doncaster Works in July 1961 after a racehorse, this being St. Paddy the winner of both the 1960 Epsom Derby and the St. Leger. Aside from eight months allocation to Haymarket (64B), this Deltic was always the responsibility of Finsbury Park. Dave Hill (D1106)*

Meanwhile the Eastern Region who had also placed orders for both of these other designs, were impressed by the capabilities of Deltic and therefore placed its own order. The theory behind the order was that although their cost was high, the 22 production Deltics would displace 57 Pacific steam engines on the region, and could therefore be expected to run an average of 4,700 to 5,000 miles per week in revenue-earning service as justification. As a consequence of the huge government investment under the 'Modernisation Plan' of the 1950s, BR were expected to heavily promote themselves as a modern system, with emphasis on speed and efficiency.

It is fair to assume, that while the Western Region was not blind to what was being achieved on the other regions, they had in the true independent fashion of Swindon, given thoughts to their own alternatives. Despite seeing the merits of the twin-engine Deltics and their higher engine running speeds, they had already made plans to supplement their 'Warship Class' diesel-hydraulics.

Above: *By 19th August 1979 55001* St. Paddy *had been put out to grass as seen in this view at Doncaster Works, although it is still carrying its nameplates. The engine had last seen work on a service train on 23rd March 1978 but it would sadly never work again, and by December it had been led to the cutting up area at the works. Officially withdrawn on 5th January 1980, the cutters set to work and it was completely demolished by the end of January that year. It should perhaps be noted that, along with 55007* Pinza, St. Paddy *was in fact on the Western Region's hallowed metals for a week in January 1975, conducting high-speed rail joint tests in connection with the introduction of HST sets.* Steven Feltham (D1107)

The Warships were only capable of 2,200hp as they were much lighter in both weight and capacity. The desire to offer faster trains to the travelling public, forced the management of the Western Region to think towards larger engines and the magical 3,000hp that would be required to achieve this.

Top Left: *Having been named at York station on 4th April 1963* The King's Own Yorkshire Light Infantry *was orinally numbered D9002. A resident of Gateshead (52A) until it was transfered to York in May 1979, we find 'KOYLI' charging through York as a light engine on 26th June 1981.*
Steve Ireland Collection (D1192)

Bottom Left: *With the East Coast Pullman stock repainted to match the blue locomotive we find 9002* The King's Own Yorkshire Light Infantry *on a hazy day at Newark on 14th July 1971. The goods yard and the signals are still very much in use at this time, whilst the permanent way hut on the right hand side adds to the scene.*
Steve Ireland Collection (D1108)

Right: The King's Own Yorkshire Light Infantry *(renumbered to 55002 in 1973) is waiting to take out the 22.30 Edinburgh service from Kings Cross on 14th December 1979. As can be seen, the brightness of the marker lights after dark is very effective. It is in night exposures such as this that we can also clearly see the interference in the classical architectural lines of Lewis Cubitt's wonderful roof design at Kings Cross, by the later additions of the catenary. Perhaps with just a little more thought (and of course money) the catenary supports could have matched the style of the vaulting supports above more sympathetically? The station was originally built for the Great Northern Railway in 1852, on what was the site of the old London Smallpox Hospital.*
Colin Whitbread (D1109)

In seeking a more powerful engine than the Warship Class, Swindon (being Swindon) went for the home-grown option and thus the 'Western' Class diesel-hydraulics were sanctioned instead. Meanwhile the Southern Region, whilst showing a passing interest in the products from English Electric for use as motive power on their Bournemouth and Exeter routes, saw that their financial resources would in fact only run to the third-rail electrification of the Bournemouth line.

Thus no further orders were placed and the fleet of Deltics on Britain's railways was limited to just the 22 production examples and the one prototype. English Electric were not to be outdone though, and because they had a spare Deltic body shell, they took the opportunity to fit it with the more economic single 16-cylinder engine.

Consequently the Diesel Prototype 2 (DP2) was up-rated to an impressive 2,700hp, with an improved 16-cylinder English Electric engine that itself could be traced back to the 1947 LMS 10000/1 design. With this they decided to try for some of the steam locomotive replacement budget from the London Midland Region.

Their new product (which later became the Class 50) was targeted at the need to upgrade services north of Crewe, where the electrification of the WCML then ended. So it was that DP2 was born into the Deltic body-shell that might have been D9022, had the order been extended. In fact it might just have easily been D1022 instead, as the original Deltics were to have been D1000 to D1021, but the management at Swindon had contrived to reserve these numbers for their own class of Western diesel hydraulics.

If all of this had transpired we could have seen a much larger fleet of Deltics, as they would not have just been confined to the East Coast Main Line. Perhaps that unforgettable sound of the engines firing up one after another could have been a regular occurrence at Glasgow Central, Waterloo and Paddington too?

Imagine for a moment, what if the funds had been available to the Western Region, would a fleet of 70+ Deltics have been created? Could this have delayed the development of the High Speed Trains or brought it forward? We can only speculate now. Yet, before I am attacked by Western enthusiasts for being biased, can I say that I am a 'Hydraulic' fan and that I hope to be covering the Western Class in another volume very soon!

In the meantime I hope you will enjoy this selection of images from the Strathwood Library and that you will be moved to make contact with us, not only to acquire duplicate slides to enhance your own collection, but also to possibly allow access to your own work, so that all can share the enjoyment of it in future publications!

We are always pleased to hear from our readers in this respect and we would also welcome ideas for subjects for the next five volumes in the Heritage Traction series. So, watch out for our advertisements for further volumes, as other classes get a similar treatment.

Kevin Derrick,   Scotland.   September 2004

Left: *Looking very much a thoroughbred at the former Great Northern Railway's London terminus in March 1967, we see D9003* Meld. *The backdrop of this famous signal box was a classic scene here until the sweeping changes of the early 1970s! New to Finsbury Park (34G),* Meld *was still on their books at this time, before an eight-month-long break in 1967/68. The engine was just a few months old at Doncaster Works in July 1961 when it was named after the winner of the 1955 St. Leger race; which of course is held annually at the nearby Doncaster Racecourse.*
Michael Beeton (D176)

Top Right: *Running fast at Hatfield on 18th March 1972, 9003* Meld *would be re-numbered the following February as 55003. Throughout most of their lives, the Deltic fleet could often be expected to 'pick up slack' from speed restrictions by anything up to 30 minutes along the entire length of the East Coast Main Line.* Dave Hill (D1110)

Bottom Right: *By the time that 55003* Meld *was crossing the path of 31199 on the approach to Kings Cross in 1979, the writing was already on the wall for the class. As we have seen, 55001 was already out of traffic and 55020 was at Doncaster.* Meld *was to be laid up from 30th December 1980 and sent to Doncaster the next day; where it was completly cut up by mid-March 1981. As these events progressed, enthusiasts around the country were actively following every movement of the class-members left in traffic.* Strathwood Library Collection (D1111)

Below: *New to Haymarket (64B) on 18th May 1961, D9004 was one of a few Deltics to run nameless for several years. This 1962 view shows it at the shed where it would remain allocated until 1979. However, a lengthy spell (from April 1978 until November 1979) was spent at Doncaster Works awaiting repairs. While a decision was made about the future, and whilst still on Doncaster Works, 55004 was temporarily transferred to York in May 1979. After being withdrawn, re-instated and withdrawn once again in late-1981, a brief trip was made to Stratford before the engine returned to York for the Christmas and New Year holidays of 1981/2. The engine was finally towed down to Doncaster in time to join the assembled engines at that famous open day in February 1982. It also has the distinction of being the last Deltic to be cut up in July 1983, a dubious honour indeed! .*
Richard Sinclair Collection (D1112)

Right: *It was not until 23rd May 1964 that D9004 was named as the* Queen's Own Highlander, *which took place in a ceremony at Inverness Station. We can see that from this 1967 picture of D9004 at Leeds Central station, that in addition to the nameplate, an attractive crest has also been fitted. However, we can clearly witness that it is still running without the repositioning of the air-horns on the bonnet of the locomotive. As can also be noted, even though the Deltics represented both a large investment and the top flight of the East Coast motive power, they were not always kept really clean. This engine was however one of eight of the class to make it to green with a full yellow front, before the main body was painted blue. This was also your author's last Deltic to 'spot' and was eventually seen some time after the rest of the class, much to my annoyance and embarrassment!*
Len Smith (D1113)

Below: *Staying in Leeds at the modernised City station in the summer of 1972, we find 9005 now 11 years old but still running very fast timings on the main lines to London from Leeds, Edinburgh and Newcastle. One of 12 of the class to be re-numbered in February 1974, it gained its name as* The Prince Of Wales's Own Regiment Of Yorkshire *in a ceremony at York station in front of dignitaries on 8th October 1963, after running nameless for over three years. New to Gateshead (52A) on 25th May 1961 it was to stay based on Tyneside until the surviving class members went* en-bloc *to York in May 1979. Withdrawn on 8th December 1981, it was taken to Doncaster on 21st February 1982 ready for the next day's Deltic Requiem at the works.*
Steve Carter Collection (D1114)

Above: *With the headcode panels plated up on most of the class by 30th January 1978, 55005* The Prince Of Wales's Own Regiment Of Yorkshire *adds to the haze on a cold afternoon in the train shed at Kings Cross after its arrival from the North. The late 1970s were to see the rapid withdrawal of many reminders of the pre-nationalised railway, and the LMS-designed 50-foot full brake parcel van behind the locomotive would be a sure fatality of this period. This policy also applied to many of the locomotive workings, especially when the HSTs began their steady incursion along the Eastern route to Scotland. Workings to Leeds and to Hull, albeit as semi-fast timings, showed the Deltic's abilities well. Your author had a very pleasurable day about this time, managing to go out and back from Kings Cross to Peterborough twice in the same day on Deltic-hauled workings. Nothing had been planned and it was just a question of having a valid ticket, then waiting to see what turned up each time. However, I do recall a discussion with an unsympathetic guard who did not like anyone standing in the corridor with a window open to enjoy the 'music'! I imagine he would have had a fit if he had found himself rostered onto an enthusiast's special!*
Ian James (D1115)

Above: *Seen during a society visit at Doncaster Works on 22nd November 1970, 9006* The Fife And Forfar Yeomanry *has all its flaps open to allow the jacking points to be accessed with lifting keys. Those with an eye for detail will notice that, prior to the TOPS repaints, the Inter City arrows were slightly larger and thicker than those later applied. Whilst this locomotive has clearly been into the shops, it has been pushed out again possibly to make room for more pressing work. Renumbered in March 1974 as 55006, this was always a Haymarket engine until the concentration of the class at York* *in May 1979. It had been given its name on 5th December 1964 in front of members of the Fife And Forfar Yeomanry regiment at Cupar in the Kingdom of Fife. The regiment includes among its Battle Honours, Gallipoli 1915, The Somme 1918 and Flanders also in 1918. This view shows it still has the attractive regimental crest in position, but officials soon decided that these crests provided too tempting a target for unscrupulous collectors so many were removed before the Deltics ended their working lives.*
John Ireland/Steve Ireland Collection (D1116)

Below: *Coupled with a chance remark from one of his band members (who was also a railway enthusiast), the sight of a Deltic at night in his native North East inspired Chris Rea to write an album track and to also name his successful album Deltics around the time of the end of the class's career. Also inspired by the sights and sounds of the Deltics was our photographer Colin Whitbread, who made many nocturnal trips to capture them on film after dark. Ready to leave Newcastle on 21st December 1979 with the 20.30 to Kings Cross on a bitterly cold night on Tyneside, we once again see 55006* The Fife And Forfar Yeomanry. *We can be sure that our photographer and other passengers on the train that night will enjoy a warm ride as the steam heating appears to be working well. After being withdrawn from stock on 8th February 1981, it arrived at Doncaster on 23rd of the same month. The task of breaking up 100-tons of locomotive took place during two weeks in July of that year.*
Colin Whitbread (D1117)

Above: *The 21.59 service from Sunderland, which combined with the 22.55 from Newcastle for Kings Cross, is waiting at York ready for the run down to London on 7th November 1980. Our train engine is 55007* Pinza, *one of the last survivors that would hang on until New Year's Eve 1981 before being taken out of Eastern Region operating stock. The engine was named after the winner of the 1953 Epsom Derby, at Doncaster station on 22nd June 1961, on what was its first day in service. As D9007 it was allocated to Finsbury Park (34G) for the next 20-years, its only break from this depot was to join* St. Paddy *on the Western Region for six days in* January 1975 for those HST track trials, Although the Western Region had allocations of Class 50s that were also passed for 100mph running, it was the acceleration of the Deltics that made them eminently more suitable for these important tests. Finally, Pinza joined the other class members as a York engine, but it still ended its career by racing up and down the East Coast Main Line in May 1981. We should note also that Pinza is wearing the white cab window surrounds once again; a trademark of Finsbury Park in their enthusiastic attempts to keep their engines looking good.*
Colin Whitbread (D1118)

Below: *Comparing the previous image with this earlier shot of 55007 taken on 26th January 1975, it reveals that a year after being re-numbered* Pinza *(like so many of the class) ran with only one number along each side of the engine. Again the earlier, slightly larger Inter City arrows are used in the period before the headcodes were plated over. For just on 20-years the Deltics were the star turns for the enthusiasts who waited at this point on the north end of the platforms at Kings Cross, as this offered the best vantage point to watch their movements back and forth as they went to or from the refuelling and servicing point. Sadly, the familiar smoke haze that grew as they accelerated in and out of Gas Works Tunnel and the old route indicators set to give the drivers the road, are all now just a distant memory.* Aldo Delicata (D1120)

Above: *This view of 55008* The Green Howards *serves as a reminder that not all of the Deltics succumbed to having their defunct headcode panels plated over or even had the benefit of marker lights being fitted. In this view from 27th February 1982 we see a stark contrast as the locomotive, awaiting its fate, has been stripped of its nameplates but has had messages of hope and affection applied in the grime. It was a contrast to what had transpired 21 years earlier, when the engine had been new into traffic on arrival from the Vulcan Works at Newton-Le-Willows. After the acceptance tests at Doncaster on 7th January 1961 it ran nameless for almost two years before it was made ready for its naming ceremony at Darlington station on 30th July 1963. The Green Howards, based at Catterick (just south of Darlington) have Ypres, The Somme, Dunkirk and Burma among their Battle Honours. Being a Gateshead engine for most of its working life, most photographs tend to show it in an unkempt condition, and thus it was following a tradition carried over from the days of the A4 steam engines before them. In May 1979 55008 became the responsibility of York, but found itself stored at Finsbury Park when the Deltic services were withdrawn on 31st December 1981. After the famous Doncaster open day, the cutters began their task of dismantling those Deltics that were not set aside for preservation including 55008. However one of the cabs was purchased privately and transported to Oxfordshire on 26th January 1982. Steve Ireland Collection (D1121)*

Top Right: *D9008* The Green Howards *had been one of the earlier repaints from green into the then new Inter City blue, but even this was getting scruffy by the time of this photograph on 12th August 1967. Interestingly the picture shows it carrying a line of dots on its headcode, as at this time the engine crews were actively using them. Whilst a feature of this scene would be more typical in a summertime view, we can see that the engine room windows have been left open to make it more comfortable for the enginemen to carry out their inspections. Also on the stabling point this day we can see a green Class 40 and a two tone Class 47. No doubt that at this time, there would still be more engines to be seen in green livery than blue.* Frank Hornby (D1122)

Bottom Right: *Having lost the D prefix and now running as 9008,* The Green Howards *had thankfully seen a repaint and had the larger arrows re-fixed when photographed at Gateshead (52A) in September 1973. Despite the clearly obvious lack of cleanliness of those engines working out of this shed, we know that it had a working engine cleaning plant as it can be seen in Volume 4 of this series (The Class 40s). Some five months after this picture was taken,* The Green Howards *became 55008 in February 1974. As an aside, can I say that I have often wondered what Deltics would have looked like had they lasted long enough to have been repainted into Large Logo livery?*
Ian King (D1123)

Below: *Performing for the crowd on the aforementioned Doncaster Deltic Day in 1982, is 55009* Alycidon. *The engine had been taken out of traffic on 2nd January, so there could have been a build-up of fuel oil in its engine bores, which would account for this splendid display of exhaust plumes when it was fired up for the amusement of the assembled photographers. This class member had picked up its name from the great racehorse and leading sire, which had won the 1949 Ascot Gold Cup and then followed up its success by winning The 1000 Guineas and The Oaks in 1952. The engine was named at Doncaster station when new to traffic on 21st July 1961, and then became another of those Deltics sent to Finsbury Park. It was to stay based in London until going to York in May 1981 to work out its last few months, although* Alycidon *did have a short six-week spell at Haymarket (64B) at the end of 1967. Thankfully this racehorse was later to leave the paddock at Doncaster for a new career in preservation.* Steve Ireland Collection (D1124)

Above: *Towards the end York's allocation of Deltics (having been displaced from the ECML), could be found working on some unusual routes after the arrival of the HSTs. This view, taken just a few days before coming out of traffic, shows 55009 Alycidon at Halifax in the snows of Sunday 27th December 1981. With just a couple of days left, the cold weather was only to spur on many photographers to get as many pictures as they could. Fortunately there were several rail tours organised during the dying days and this is one of them. Complete with headboards and a wreath* Alycidon *certainly looks in fine fettle as it threads through the snow. The class's swansong years working on the trans-Pennine routes may be considered by some to be a 'relegation', yet they were well suited to these duties, as their combined 36 cylinders could easily cope with the severe gradients on the routes between Yorkshire and Lancashire.* Ian Harrison (D1125)

Above: *In a lovely tranquil scene at Offord in the Vale of York our next Deltic, 55010 The King's Own Scottish Borderer, is seen on 20th September 1978 running close to the course of the River Ouse. Allocated when new on 24th July 1961 to Haymarket (64B), it was perhaps fitting that the name of a Scottish regiment should be chosen. However, it was not until 8th May 1965 before D9010 arrived at Dumfries to be named after the South of Scotland's famous regiment. This regiment's Battle Honours included Arnhem 1944 and Korea in 1951-2, but its history can be traced back to 1689. The fuel tanks seen to advantage in this view carried 826 gallons, whilst others had to carry up to 640 gallons of water for the steam heat boiler as well. This broadside position also shows that the leading side windows on the cabs of Deltics were plated over as a modification of the mid-1970s. Along with 9013 The Black Watch and 9016 Gordon Highlander, 9010 was among the last three of the class to be re-numbered on the week ending 22nd June 1974. The distinction of being the first of the class to gain the new numbers was 9020 Nimbus in the week ending 11th November 1973. Ian James (D1126)*

Below: *Newcastle-upon-Tyne is the setting for another night scene, this time on 27th November 1981. Again we feature 55010* The King's Own Scottish Borderer, *which has command of the 20.00 Kings Cross - Aberdeen sleeper service, during its last few weeks in operation. As can be seen in the foreground, facilities were provided at Newcastle for locomotives to take on water for their steam heat boilers. Transferred away from Haymarket for the first and last time in May 1979, it went to York. It was from here that it was switched off on Christmas Eve 1981 after travelling light engine to Doncaster; by the third week of May 1982 it was reduced to scrap at the works. It was also (unfortunately) among those of the regimental Deltics to lose its crests as seen in both of these shots, the very first being another class member named after a Scottish regiment,* The Black Watch. Colin Whitbread (D1127)

Above: *Just occasionally the chance of seeing a pair of Deltics double-heading could be found along the East Coast Mainline. This was not because two Class 55s were needed for one train, but usually because one of them had failed. This was possibly the case where 55011* The Royal Northumberland Fusiliers *had expired and 55012* Crepello *was on hand as a standby. Whatever the reason, the pair makes a stirring sight when seen awaiting the road at Selby in 1979. D9011 was sent to Gateshead (52A) when new on 20th August 1961, to help oust the last of the Pacific steam locomotive types from the depot. It was later selected to become* The Royal Northumberland Fusiliers *and received the endorsement of the regiment in a ceremony at Newcastle Central station on 28th May 1963.*

The locomotive remained allocated to Gateshead until May 1979 when it also joined others in becoming a York engine. As a celebration of York, the depot there began affixing small transfers showing the City's coat of arms above the locomotive numbers and these can be seen in more detail on page 58. As The Royal Northumberland Fusiliers *was not to be given a crest or badge above the nameplate, the crest of York would have to suffice. Interestingly, this view makes another statement about BR policy in the late-1970s, as there seems to be no hard and fast rule about whether the TOPS number should be used once or twice on the sides of the class, as witnessed here by the difference in this consecutively numbered pairing.* Paul Senior/Leonard Ball Collection (D1128)

Above: *Doncaster's famous works, seen here in the background, was where the Deltic class members received their major overhauls, although other work was carried out on the depots and sometimes at Stratford Works as well. Several types of DMUs (and different paint schemes) are also to be seen in the picture, as 55011 The Royal Northumberland Fusiliers takes the 12.05 Kings Cross to Hull north from Doncaster on 28th May 1980. Their use on these turns certainly improved* *the journey times and the loadings of these trains as enthusiasts took advantage of Deltic haulage. Taken out of service on 8th November 1981, 55011 went to Stratford Works first of all, before finally moving northwards to the Doncaster Plant on the 23rd of the month. It then lingered around the works yard waiting its turn for cutting, which did not come until November 1982.*
Colin Whitbread (D1129)

Above: *Our next class member, 9012* Crepello, *arrives at Kings Cross on 4th May 1971, but our photographer seems to have fallen foul of one of the gangers working on the complex pointwork. The ganger's gesturing serves to remind us that we should always be careful, even when standing on the platform edge. Taking up the name of a racehorse after its acceptance trials at Doncaster Works on 4th September 1961,* Crepello *was a long-term favourite for spotters in the capital. The name was taken from the winner of the 1957 Epsom Derby and this engine certainly proved to be a racehorse as it had a prestigious and distinctive presence along the length of the route between the capitals of England and Scotland for 20 years. Again it was based at Finsbury Park for almost its entire career, apart from a brief spell of four months that it spent at Haymarket in 1968.*

Although the modern trains may well be faster, for many enthusiasts they do not have the same allure. If one compares the background of page 8 and the picture of D9003 Meld *at the same location, they will notice that the new Kings Cross power box has sprung up in the intervening four years by the York Road platform that gave access to 'The Drain' and the widened lines towards Moorgate. This new box is then seen again in the background on page 9. Once completed it allowed the removal of that landmark box (seen in nearly all Kings Cross shots from the steam and early diesel eras) along with a host of splendid smaller signal boxes at the southern end of the East Coast Mainline. Needless to say the view here today is quite different and the occasional passage of goods trains, between the locals in and out of 'The Drain' is no more.*
Michael Beeton (D174)

Below: Crepello *was re-numbered in February 1974 as 55012, but this view shows the inconvenience to 'spotters' trying to catch numbers at speed or for photographers, especially when the single number on each side was found at the wrong end. We see the engine ready for the 'off' at Kings Cross on 20th May 1980, the suitably prepared headboard shows it taking advantage of the soon to be withdrawn Pullman stock on a special that will head first to Scarborough. For this event the paintwork has been cleaned, it is oiled up along the flanks to gain some shine, and the paint has been touched up as well it seems. Along with details around the buffer beams,* Crepello *has scrubbed up well for the occasion. Removed from service on 19th May 1981 and sent to Doncaster on 15th June,* Crepello *was completely cut up by the second week of September. Sadly missed, the Deltics were nevertheless a fitting tribute to British enterprise, as they certainly proved that English Electric's gamble with* Deltic *well and truly paid off!* Colin Whitbread (D1130)

Top Left: *The unfortunate distinction of being the first Deltic to lose its crests above the nameplates seems to have fallen upon 9013* The Black Watch, *as witnessed in this shot at Kings Cross on 22nd July 1973. It adopted the name of one of the most famous army regiments in the world in a ceremony at Dundee West station on 12th January during the severe winter of 1963. It is a matter of military history that the Black Watch are regarded as the most senior of the Highland Regiments and the sole wearers of the famous Red Hackle since the 1770s. When new the engine was sent to Doncaster Works from the English Electric factory at Newton-le-Willows via the Woodhead route and was actually watched passing through Penistone station by my editor. After its acceptance trials, it went into service on a much warmer day - 14th August 1961. The original cab windows are still very much in place in this our first shot of the engine.* Brian Ireland/Steve Ireland Collection (D1131)

Bottom Left: *Caught once more at Kings Cross, 55013* The Black Watch *has gained the headcodes and the cab window modifications by 1978. Originally when built, the entire class were fitted with vacuum braking and steam heat only, but these specifications were later upgraded to dual air/vacuum braking, together with steam and electric heating equipment. Thus they were able to deal with the improved MkII coaching stock that came into service in the early 1970s.* Strathwood Library Collection (D1132)

Above: *By the time of the rundown of the class, several were to receive additional paint details as seen by the roof panels and fuel tanks on 55013* The Black Watch *leaving Doncaster for Hull with the 08.05 service from Kings Cross on 25th May 1980. This level of detailing is to be found on the buffer beams and the bogies, with fitters taking the time to paint the springs and sand pipes also. The background to the picture reveals that several Cravens DMUs and one of the class 97/7 battery locomotives converted from London District 501 stock are at the works for attention. We have often mentioned that the works were the main repair centre for the Deltic class, but a little about its unique history would not go amiss either. Originally the main locomotive repair works of the Great Northern Railway was built at Boston on the Lincolnshire coast before 1853. However, it was the persuasion of the local MP Edmund Beckett Denison and the close proximity of large coalfields and centres of iron-founding that led the Board of the GNR to change the location. The first locomotive to actually be built at this 'new' works at Doncaster, which became known later as 'The Plant', was a little 0-4-2 locomotive in 1867. Once in its stride the works went on to build and design some of the most famous steam engine types including Patrick Stirling's GNR singles and what are arguably known as the world's most famous engines, the LNER's* Mallard *and* Flying Scotsman.

Colin Whitbread (D1133)

Above: *Having come to a standstill under one of the old and distinctive water cranes that used to adorn the station canopies at Newcastle Central station, we see 9014* The Duke Of Wellington's Regiment *on 30th March 1972. This was one of the last of the Deltic fleet to be re-painted into blue from green in November 1969. As D9014 it had acquired the name in a ceremony at Darlington station on 22nd October 1963 when just over two years old. This name was acquired from a famous Yorkshire regiment, who are not just the only army unit to carry four colours when on parade but also have had ten*

Victoria Crosses awarded to those soldiers who have served with it. A reference back to the 1972 Ian Allan British Railways Locoshed Book (now including the Locoshed Directory *for the first time), suggests that the walk from Newcastle Central station to Gateshead (52A) could be completed in 15 minutes across the Low Level Bridge. What it did not mention was just how cold this walk over the River Tyne could be on a winter's day, as no doubt many of our readers will be able to testify.*

Brian Lowe/Steve Ireland Collection (D1134)

Below: *As mentioned previously, the last year of the Deltics brought cameramen out in great numbers to record what they could. This splendid view at Doncaster on 4th April 1981 shows what the intrepid photographer could achieve, for with the cab lights and a figure in the distance, the train stands in a haze as the escaping steam-heating vapour mixes with the cold night air. This Kings Cross train is the combined 21.59 Sunderland, 22.55 Newcastle and 00.50 Leeds services that met up at Doncaster for the very early morning run to Kings Cross. Inside a few months the engine would be back in Doncaster, although it would not be making any more runs south (or north come to that) as by 22nd November, 55014 was out of service. The engine would linger around the works for almost another year before finally being reported as cut up by 16th February 1982. This meant that by the date of the Deltic Open day held at Doncaster two weeks later, little trace of 55014 would be left.*

Colin Whitbread (D1135)

Top Left: *Moving on to our next member of the fleet, we reach 9015* Tulyar, *seen at Kings Cross on 11th July 1970. This was among the last of the Deltics left in green livery, despite the fact that this paint scheme was starting to get faded by this date. In this picture we see its driver backing cautiously onto what looks to be a shorter than normal express for the West Riding that summer (at least judging from the positioning of the locomotive in the platforms). The Brute trolley seen on the left-hand-side brings back happy memories of my sitting on these useful mobile seats not only at this location, but at many other places as well. Of course, the porters would leave them where they needed them later, but we enthusiasts would move them to where we got a better view.*
Ian James (D1169)

Bottom Left: Tulyar, *was one of the Deltics that became a regular for photographers in that last year! This was always an easy class member to identify because of the plaque on its headcode panels. Named after the winner of both the 1952 St. Leger and the Epsom Derby,* Tulyar's *nameplates were applied when new at Doncaster Works on 13th October 1961. We see it first after dark at Peterborough on Thursday 5th March 1981, having arrived with the 17.12 Kings Cross to Peterborough service. Still carrying the white cab roof details first applied by Finsbury Park (34G), it may well remind some of our readers of the earlier days of the Baby Deltics.*
Colin Whitbread (D1136)

Below: *With the end fast approaching, we join those on the 'Deltic Queen of Scots' Rail Tour for the photo stop at Grantham on 7th November 1981, and note that since becoming a York engine* Tulyar's *attractive white cab surrounds have been painted over in blue once again. This Deltic was very fortunate indeed, for having had a fire on board at Leuchars six days later, it was a very likely candidate for withdrawal and scrapping. Yet it was to join those preserved machines by being repaired after appearing in the line of Deltics at the Works Open Day as seen on Page 60, where the white cab surrounds have been restored again! The 'Queen of Scots Pullman' service originally began in 1928, linking London Kings Cross with both Edinburgh Waverley and Glasgow Queen Street. It was the arrival of the Deltics on this service in the early 1960s that put many of those steam engines also with racehorse names out to grass, perhaps it is therefore poetic that it was adopted for one of the Deltic's last enthusiasts specials. Steve Ireland Collection (D1137)*

Above: *I have mentioned quite a number of naming ceremonies already but some, like the one afforded D9016 Gordon Highlander at Aberdeen station on 28th July 1964 were quite lavish. With the nearside nameplates still covered over, the engine is moved into position under the watchful gaze of a boy scout. We can see that despite the locomotive being nearly three years into its service life, the trouble that had been* taken to provide a suitable red carpet, whilst the canopy above the dignitaries had been painted to brighten up the sooty station. Also present and in steam on this day, was the ex-LNER Class D49 4-4-0 which also carried the name *Gordon Highlander; however, to the railwaymen in the Highlands the steam engine was always known as 'The Soldier'.*
Dr Tommy Simpson (D164)

Top Right: *With no thoughts whatsoever of the class even coming out of traffic, we see 9016* Gordon Highlander *on 25th August 1973 at the head of a service for Grimsby and Cleethorpes (if the headcode is to be believed). Sent new to Haymarket it was to stay based in Edinburgh for most of its career, aside from that period in late 1967 and early 1968 when the original allocation of the class was briefly swapped around. It later spent nine months out of use at Doncaster Works in 1979 and was then re-allocated to York in May of that year whilst still on the works. Its working days on British Rail officially came to an end on 30th December 1981.* Brian Ireland/Steve Ireland Collection (D1138)

Bottom: *Making a then rare appearance at Barrow Hill for the Open Day held there on 7th October 1979, we find 55016* Gordon Highlander *with the steam heating boiler apparently working well. We also see that those larger style arrows are being used in the livery scheme but that only one running number is seen on each side. As a point of interest, I have noted during the compilation of this volume how many times these appeared on engines. With six of the original 22 service engines and the prototype all having survived into preservation, we are indeed fortunate that we can still enjoy these fine engines today. Their appearances at preserved railway diesel galas or on mainline rail tours always gathers a crowd of enthusiasts and photographers.* Colin Whitbread (D1139)

Above: *This view at Selby makes an excellent comparison with the picture shown earlier in this book as even these 'modern' style of station lamps seen there have in turn been replaced across the network with newer designs. However the chance of catching the sight and sounds of a Deltic on the through lines was one not to be missed at this location. In this case we are rewarded with the passage of 55017* The Durham Light Infantry *on 8th July 1978. At Selby, 174 miles from Kings Cross, a speed restriction of 40mph is required across the famous swing bridge that spans the River Ouse. Once over the river, a thunderous roar would sound out as the distinctive Deltic engines opened out yet again. We find it to be remarkably clean for a Gateshead engine, for as stated this shed was not known for the pristine condition of its engines. It was to continue in service with the Eastern Region until the last day of 1981, when it was then stored briefly at Finsbury Park, before travelling to join its classmates for breaking up at Doncaster Works.* Leonard Ball (D1140)

Below: *New to British Railways as D9017 on 10th November 1961, this Deltic ran anonymously until 29th October 1963, when the nameplates of* The Durham Light Infantry *were unveiled. This splendid name had been carried since 1958 by Class V2 2-6-2 60964, but two other V2s also carried names that were later taken on in one form or another by Deltics, including 60872* King's Own Yorkshire Light Infantry, *taken up by D9002, and 60835 which gave up the name* The Green Howard, Alexandra, Princess Of Wales's Own Yorkshire Regiment *for the simpler version on D9008. We are reminded that the 'DLI' fought in every major battle in World War I, with over 13,000 Durham men falling in the field during 'the war to end all wars'.*

At the former London depot whilst they had their own allocation of Deltics, the preferred names were usually of racehorses rather than the regiments. We catch D9017 The Durham Light Infantry *in the lines on shed at Finsbury Park (34G) in 1965. Visiting Deltics from Gateshead and Haymarket such as D9017* The Durham Light Infantry, *were usually turned around at Kings Cross stabling point for fuelling purposes rather than take up valuable line occupation through both the Gasworks and Copenhagen tunnels and make the two mile long climb to the depot at Finsbury Park. Therefore the appearance here was possibly for something mechanical that needed to be carried out before it returned home.* Simon Combe (D160)

Top Left: *Carrying the splendid name of* Ballymoss *after the racehorse that won the St. Leger in 1957, D9018 is seen at Leeds City on 16th November 1967. It was taken into service with this name from new on 24th November 1961 and went to London's Finsbury Park depot, where it was based until May 1981. A decision to withdraw the engine was made on 13th October 1981, and it passed to Stratford in East London to be stripped of usable spares. It arrived back at the Doncaster Works one day short of 20 years since it had entered service! It was sent to the cutting position to be gone by 30th January and had thus become just another memory by the time of the Deltic Open Day on 27th February 1982.* Paul Barber (D1141)

Bottom Left: *In happier times we see the now renumbered 55018* Ballymoss *with larger Inter City arrows in place, although its cab window surrounds are now painted blue. It also has an unusual marker dot application to the headcode panels with smaller dots when it was caught on film as it carried out the usual stabling point shuffle at Kings Cross in 1975. At this time the cab windows were yet to be modified, although it had been re-numbered with the earlier standard 'one number each side' in February 1974. Sometimes the visitor to the platform's end at this location would be treated to an engine movement every few minutes during busy periods, especially when the yard was full. So those engines that blocked the earlier arrivals had to be moved to let them back out.*
Roger Griffiths (D1142)

Above: *In the final shot from this trio of images of D9018/55018, we see that the Finsbury Park trademark of white surrounds have been restored. We should also refer the reader back to page 10 where D9004 carries a differing pattern above the roofline. Although* Ballymoss *has received the attentions of the painters, it has been missed by the cleaners as evidenced on arrival at Leeds City on 11th March 1981. We can also see that as part of the Finsbury Park treatment, it has acquired two numbers on either side once again. The opaque marker lights glow nicely in the twilight, as it waits with the 16.05 Liverpool to Newcastle working. Even from a distance, the sound of those Deltic engines running at speed, coupled with the powerful nose profile and the distinctive horn note, identified one of these locomotives as being a Deltic long before it came fully into sight. Whilst they had been relegated from the principle express workings, these twin-engined diesels seemed to thrive on the hard work they faced on the gradients of the trans–Pennine route and its more frequent stopping and starting of trains. The single-engined English Electric-built nine-cylinder locomotives, understandably nicknamed the 'Baby Deltics' (TOPS Class 23), in a lighter Bo-Bo configuration, were a pale comparison of their bigger brothers. Aside from the lower maximum speed of just 75mph, their reliability with the stop-start trains on the London outer suburban duties was dubious to say the least. Faced with a steady climb out of London with commuter-laden evening trains (with on average seven BR MkI coaches or the BR-built 56-foot suburban coaches trailing behind), their acceleration did not set the world alight. However a full-blown Deltic with eight coaches on a trans-Pennine working even in their twilight years was quite something else!*
Colin Whitbread (D1143)

Above: *Taken as a pleasant record of the Royal Border Bridge before the disfiguring application of catenary, we can recall the days of the Deltics on this wonderful structure. This 28-arch viaduct was built to cross the River Tweed at Berwick by Robert Stephenson between 1847 and 1850, and was officially opened by Queen Victoria. Running 126 feet above the river is 55019* Royal Highland Fusilier, *with the 05.50 Kings Cross to Aberdeen on 27th January 1981.This was the last of the class to receive a name in a ceremony at Glasgow Central station on 11th November 1965, nearly four years after it entered service at Haymarket (64B). A Battle Honour is a token of the Sovereign's recognition of distinguished action and the Royal Highland Fusiliers possess more than two hundred such honours; a record which is unsurpassed by any other regiment in the British Isles. Among these many honours is one for Waterloo.* Colin Whitbread (D1144)

Top Right: *Seen arriving at Kings Cross in 1968, we see D9019* Royal Highland Fusilier *with a rake of mixed-livery Pullmans. This angle of the station looking across from the York Road platforms shows how so much has changed during the era of the Deltics. For instance the track layout was considerably simplified, and as we have mentioned elsewhere in this book, a new power box has since been positioned at this spot. Sadly this was not, as far as I know, a common angle for photographers, and now the opportunity has gone forever. The engine displays a heavy exhaust, probably because of being checked by signals between the Gasworks Tunnel and the station throat.*
John Green (D1145)

Bottom Right: *Now having lost the D prefix to become 9019, we see* Royal Highland Fusilier *running at the head of MkII coaching stock while making a stop at Doncaster in 1973. This was a long established stop at Doncaster, and prior to the Grouping of 1923 it had marked the boundary between two ECML partners. This was where the Great Northern Railway handed over the care of through trains to the North Eastern Railway, although the actual boundary between the two companies was at Shaftholme Junction a few miles north of the station. November of 1973 would see this engine receive the TOPS number of 55019 and it would retain this until the last day of 1981, when the locomotive went to Doncaster Works before being sold into preservation.*
Roger Griffiths (D1146)

Top Left: *Running into York station non-stop from Edinburgh, and crossing over the former North Eastern Railway lines heading towards Scarborough, D9020 is seen on 3rd May 1967. The various junctions of lines around York were incorporated into one of the earliest power box schemes in the world, which relied on over 5,000 little light bulbs to show the paths and positions of the trains under the control of the signalmen. These signalmen had 827 different combinations of track routes at their fingertips in the early 1960s. This is the third station to be built at York, the first only lasting a few years in that great expansion of the new railway era and closing in 1841, whilst the second was superseded by the present station in 1877.*
Mick Farrer (D1147)

Bottom Left: *Prior to leaving Doncaster Works to take up its duties on 12th February 1962,* Nimbus *had been named after the racehorse that won the 1949 Epsom Derby. The locomotive then went to Finsbury Park for the whole of its service life, which was to be the shortest of all of the production Deltics. It was laid up at Doncaster from 26th April 1978 until December 1979, when it was moved to the cutting area. It was then officially withdrawn on 5th January 1980 and quickly reduced to just the cabs by the end of the month. It is seen here having beaten the 1958 Brush-built A1A-A1A (Class 31) 31015 to the executioners' block. This Type 2 would provide the next week's work for the scrapmen,*
Steve Ireland Collection (D1180)

42

Below: *It is interesting to draw comparisons in the lettering styles used on the Deltic class members, and this shot from 14th June 1968 allows us to do just that. Here we see a now blue D9020* Nimbus *in the company of a green-liveried D9017* The Durham Light Infantry, *as they stand together between duties at Kings Cross. Also of note is the fact that there are two chromed makers plates each side under the cab windows. The locomotives being left with doors and windows open might be considered a problem today, but access for enthusiasts and cameraman to the stabling point at Kings Cross was almost unheard of back then. In fact I have seen very little photographic material taken at the stabling point aside from the traditional views from the platforms, or back down from the road bridge above the Gasworks Tunnel. Over the years needless to say the various shed directories and depot guides have scantily passed over this stabling point, as access was only really across the busy network of tracks from the platforms. So unless they were among the extremely privileged few visitors (or British Railways paid their wages) the average photographer would have had to run the gauntlet of a large number of railwaymen to reach this location; not to mention the chance of falling foul of the Railway Police who also had their offices at Kings Cross and were never far away.*
Frank Hornby (D1148)

Above: *The two 'open day' shots on pages 44 and 45 (taken nine years apart), allow some of the differences in appearance and preparation standards to be assessed. Our first view shows 9021 Argyll & Sutherland Highlander on display and getting the once over from a young lassie at Eastfield (65A) in September 1972. The last Deltic into service on 2nd May 1962, D9021 ran without dedication until 29th November 1963 when it was bestowed with honours at a naming ceremony in Stirling station. Nine years later it is still fitted with its regimental badges, as it stands proud on parade; and well it should for the regiment after which it was named can claim 16 Victoria Crosses, six of them being awarded in the same campaign at Lucknow in India in 1857. Many of our readers will recall with fond memories their own first sighting of one of these magnificent machines. Your author's was of this engine greeting him after running in excitement up to the top of the steps leading from the London Transport Underground station; there stood D9021 with its Deltic engines throbbing away having just arrived from the North, at Kings Cross.*
Arthur Wilson (D1149)

Below: *Clearly, by the time of 55021's guest appearance at Stratford's Open Day on 11th July 1981 not only were standards slipping, but three of the class had already been cut up! A fourth (55006) was also being reduced to scrap at this time at Doncaster, so the end was not too far away. Now a resident of York,* Argyll & Sutherland Highlander *bears the city's coat of arms above its number and the depot-coding sticker YK below the data panel. Removed from operating stock on 31st December 1981, it moved to Doncaster a week later. The cutters found their way to 55021 the following September, but one full cab was sold for private preservation at the time. Within another 20 years both Stratford and York depots would be closed and consigned to history, each having been home to previously large locomotive allocations in both the steam and the early diesel eras. Although Doncaster was the main works for the upkeep of the class, from time to time in the 1970s Deltics would appear in the Stratford Works for those light repairs that were beyond the scope of the depots. This familiarity would bear fruit as Stratford then took on the task of cannibalising some locomotives as their time expired, in order to supply valuable components to keep the surviving class members moving. This work also kept employment going a while longer in an ever-contracting railway, as the few jobs that survived at Stratford Works in Mrs. Thatcher's Britain were in very sharp contrast to the workforce of over two thousand at the time of the nationalisation of the railways in 1948, certainly not a case of jobs for the boys!*

Aldo Delicata (D1150)

Above: *It is perhaps fitting that the first of the class D9000, later renumbered as 55022 after April 1974, should still be there at the end. Indeed it was still carrying its nameplates as* Royal Scots Grey, *although the badges had been removed, when the engine was pictured on 2nd January 1982 with that final tour train at Edinburgh Waverley. So it was the longest in active service, having been new from Vulcan Foundry in January 1961, although it remained at the maker's works for testing while D9001 went to Doncaster for acceptance. This engine went into service on 28th February 1961, five days after D9001. Its naming as* Royal Scots Grey, *after the famous regiment that fought at Blenheim, Waterloo and Balaklava, was the second 'railway use' of the name as a former LMS Royal Scot 4-6-0 (46101) had previously paid tribute to the regiment.* Leonard Ball (D1151)

Right: *Bearing the number D9000 and still resplendent with its badges on 25th January 1969, we find the doyen of the class in company with three other class members whilst standing around at Kings Cross, as they waited for workings back to the north again. This view shows that Haymarket engines regularly worked the full length between the two capitals and that they did so without the fitting of corridor connections. These nose-cone doors had been a feature of many of the earlier English Electric D200 series (1Co-Co1 design) diesels, later Class 40. In their absence the Deltics could not work non-stop from London to Edinburgh, although this had been the proud boast of the East Coast service back in the days of BR steam. Instead the schedules had to be revised to allow a crew change en-route after a stop was made, often on the centre roads at Doncaster.* Frank Hornby (D1152)

Left: *In this working from Liverpool Lime Street on 4th November 1981, we can see that a rendition of an earlier style of numbering (D9000) has been applied, as well as the correct 55022 on* Royal Scots Grey. *The grey/silver painted roof panels can be seen to advantage as the charismatic twin plumes of exhaust are sent skywards. As was often the case in these last weeks of Deltic operations, a group of enthusiasts has gathered to watch the departure, others will no doubt ride the train. Thus we have come full circle as the prototype's first trials were on London Midland Region metals from Liverpool some 26 years earlier. By the time of this view however, flats now overlook the city's main station along with offices built during the late-1960s, whilst the long awaited electrification catenary is also finally in place.*
Strathwood Library Collection (D1153)

Above: *The honour of being the first diesel into a blue livery and running on British Railways was to befall the prototype Deltic on 13th December 1955, when* Deltic *officially commenced working from Liverpool Edge Hill depot. It had in fact been on test from the Dick Kerr Works of English Electric in Preston since October 1955. By July 1959 most of the testing was completed on the London Midland Region and it was running on the Eastern Region, where we find the prototype on Gamston Bank in 1960. Sadly the locomotive suffered a major engine failure in 1961 and after much debate by English Electric as to whether to repair the engine for trials in Canada, it was instead sent to the Science Museum in London in 1963. It now resides in the National Railway Museum at York, so close to where the last allocation of Deltics was based.* Trans-Pennine Archive (D1154)

Above: *I cannot be sure whether all the Deltics entered service without the yellow warning panels, however those that were in service seem to have enjoyed two British Railways totems on either side of the locomotive once they had been named. This is illustrated by D9009 Alycidon in August 1961 in a view taken at York just days after it entered service (note the silvered buffers). As this picture quite readily demonstrates, the original livery on the Deltics featured the two-tone green colour scheme, but some commentators have said that this was not very distinctive in the dark or failing light, and worse still in foggy weather. Readers often ask us about the actual colours of the green paintwork on skirting, but this appears to vary according to the light and the film stocks used in these pictures, which it has to be remembered are now over 40-years old.*
Richard Sinclair Collection (D1155)

Top Right: *It appears equally certain that many of the class were given the new warning panels in yellow fairly quickly, as seen on D9006 at Darlington Works in 1963. The larger central totem would, needless to say, foul any nameplates and the line of grilles and windows above gave little choice in the placing of the totems. This is also a reminder that D9006 was not named as* The Fife And Forfar Yeomanry *until late 1964. Another fact emerges from this view in that, until its complete closure in 1966, Darlington Works had shared some of the lighter repairs on the class. The works was in fact quite capable of working on diesels and built a fair number itself after the initial trial orders had been placed at other BR works.* Colin Bowen (D154)

Bottom Right: *The application of warning panels on the front of diesels had been decided upon after a spate of accidents in East Anglia, with diesels coming upon track gangs or level crossings more quietly than the steam engines they had replaced. The panels got progressively larger and finally covered the entire nose cone or front of an engine. This increased safety feature is witnessed on D9003* Meld, *whilst it is in charge of the up Midlothian service at York on 3rd May 1967. It would appear from studying photographs that at least nine of the class made it to this livery including D9001/5/6/10/14/15/17/18. Inevitably the time taken to repaint the new corporate image of the late 1960s onto all the locomotives and rolling stock would take its time. This led to an interesting period of liveries but it was caught in the unfortunate 'gap' that occurred when many cameramen ceased taking shots after August 1968.* Mick Farrer (D1156)

Above: *Oddly enough, no sooner had most of British Rail's fleet of locomotives been re-painted into the corporate blue colour scheme, than there began to appear several celebrity re-paints back into representations of the earlier liveries. One such example for the Deltics was seen with 55002* The King's Own Yorkshire Light Infantry *at Edinburgh Waverley, after the engine was outshopped in this livery from Doncaster a few weeks earlier following its last classified repairs in 1980.*
Strathwood Library Collection (D1157)

Right: *Perhaps the real rare 'oddball' in green livery was D9010* The King's Own Scottish Borderers, *which had a localised repaint to the numbers and application of the Inter City arrows. We find the locomotive in question lurking on the stabling point at Kings Cross surrounded by Brush products and another unknown Deltic (still with a half-yellow front) tantalisingly at the back. This undated shot would have been taken in late 1968 or early 1969.*
Win Wall/Strathwood Library Collection (SH208)

Above: *Various 'Flying Scotsman' headboards have appeared over the years, but certainly the most attractive to many eyes was the winged thistle variety. Bringing this famous train towards its journey's end at Kings Cross in 1965 we find D9006* The Fife And Forfar Yeomanry. *These stylish headboards were cast in fibreglass and painted gold, and they certainly gave the train that little bit of extra status during the short period they were used in the mid-1960s. For the record the distance from Kings Cross to Edinburgh Waverley via the ECML was 392 miles. As previously mentioned, even though the Deltics reduced the actual timings on this most famous of trains, they could not run this service non-stop without a crew change en-route. This locomotive carries the same application of the light grey window and dark grey roof as seen on D9004 in both shots earlier in this volume, the angle of the photograph shows the red buffer beam to be more prominent than the yellow. The yellow-painted Timken roller bearing axle box covers (as seen throughout this book) tended to become almost black in appearance under the oily grime of everyday service.* Len Smith (D1158)

Below: *When considering some of the headboards carried by the class through their lives, we might consider that the one worn here by 55022/D9000 Royal Scots Grey takes the biscuit. Here the engine is passing through Clay Cross on the Midland route south of Sheffield, en-route from York to Paddington with a chartered special on 28th November 1981. Certainly everything except the bogies has been cleaned up for this working. In contrast, the sunlight on the bogies highlights the everyday surface rust and brake dust. Ironically, although Deltics were very rare around this location in their active service days, preservation has given some of the survivors a firm foothold in the area today.*

One thing I chose not to cover in this book was Deltics in their preserved guise, and for the purists among us certainly not pictures of them in a purple livery! This is as garish as I wish to go in this volume of Heritage Traction; *we will leave the multi-coloured swap shop liveries to later books on Class 47s and 37s. I might just consider for a moment what the names of additional Deltics might have been if the sales force of English Electric had been more successful, might the Western Region have continued with a Warship theme, or even have fallen back to using the names of Kings or stately homes, and would the London Midland Region have perpetuated the names of its Duchess Class?* Ian Harrison (D1159)

Above: *Something in the way of a more traditional special headboard was created for the Deltic Preservation Society's 'Deltic 20th Anniversary' working, which is seen waiting to leave Kings Cross behind 55022. Here Royal Scots Grey is showing a battered nose and classmate 55021 Argyll & Sutherland Highlander also ran for a while in 1979 with a similar bashed nose. Although it is certainly raining, this locomotive seems to have only one windscreen wiper fitted on each of the cab screens, while the picture of Meld opposite shows two wipers per screen working in the rain.*
Strathwood Library Collection (D1160)

Top Right: *Getting a split decision from the judges for the scruffiest Deltic in service days whilst working a train, could go to 55012 Crepello at Doncaster with the 07.05 Edinburgh-Kings Cross on 29th December 1978 in the rain.*
Leonard Ball (D1161)

Bottom Right: *Or maybe you would judge 55003 Meld (also from Finsbury Park and caught in the rain on the same day at Doncaster whilst heading the 09.00 Kings Cross-Hull) as the dirtiest working Deltic!*
Leonard Ball (D1162)

BADGES, CRESTS AND NAMEPLATES

Top Left: *Showing us what it is like at the controls of a 3,300hp diesel, we have a view from the driver's position of 55015* Tulyar *in 1981. The Automatic Warning System (AWS) is clearly level with the driver's eye-line. The almost simple-looking nature of the dials and switches when compared to modern cars with a fraction of the power beggars belief. Although the class were upgraded and modified at various times in their service lives, they were essentially using 1950s technology whilst working on a railway that was busy selling the concept of HSTs; obviously something had to give!* Matthew Hall (D1163)

Middle Left: *Many of the Deltics that were allocated to York after 1979 gained the city's coat of arms as an embellishment. That magic maximum speed of 100 mph only shared by the Class 50s in the diesel fleet is clearly visible in the warning panel. This view also reveals that quite a few body-side repairs have been made over the years, most likely following a shunting accident. Such minor collisions occurred as an engine struck a badly placed wagon, coach or another locomotive that had been left too close to points in a crowded depot after dark. When considering the safety record of the Deltics, the only accident to bring fatalities was as a result of excessive speed. This occurred on 7th May 1969, when a Kings Cross - Aberdeen Sleeping Car service approached a 40mph section at Morpeth in Northumberland at twice the permitted speed. The driver of D9011 (ironically)* The Royal Northumberland Fusiliers *mistook his location and the sleeping cars behind were derailed at a cost of six lives. The incident did, however, bring about the universal application of the Adwance Warning System (AWS) on British Rail.* Strathwood Library Collection (D1164)

Bottom Left: *As already mentioned and seen as an adornment to the front of 55015* Tulyar, *was this special plate, now shown in detail. Several other diesels appeared at the Rainhill celebrations, including a Class 25 and a Class 56. Whilst one was still almost new, the others did not carry the same level of enthusiastic following to be awarded similar plaques.* Matthew Hall (D1165)

Top Right: *The only class member to carry this style of chromed nameplate was 55008* The Green Howards. *It also appears to have carried one of the largest badges as well. This view was taken in 1981, and shows it carried its colours to the end! Sadly, many photographers missed their chance for views without the often-damaged boltholes and thus reveal where a proud crest had once been displayed. These polished regimental badges were carried by D9000/6/8/10/13/16/19 and D9021. Another mishap also befell 55008, on 16th February 1977 on the 08.00 service from Kings Cross to Edinburgh, when it struck an empty DMU at Darlington, although no serious damage was sustained. This was yet another cruel coincidence, as this engine was named at Darlington.*
Matthew Hall (D1166)

Middle Right: *Those Deltics named after racehorses didn't carry any badges or emblems. As typical of this style of nameplate I have chosen 55018* Ballymoss *seen in 1978. Considering the later changes in public attitudes it is perhaps just as well the authorities did not decide on naming Deltics after famous hunts with cast brass foxes as they had done with the London North Eastern Railways D49 4-4-0s. Such a controversial policy may well have caused the kind of problems that were witnessed with A4 60009* Union of South Africa, *which reverted to its original name of* Osprey *whilst the issue of apartheid was pointedly in the world's political forum. I wonder if the Eastern Region ever did consider perpetuating its bird theme from the early days of the A4s, but later decided that the other traditional Eastern Region theme of naming engines after racehorses gave more mileage?*
Aldo Delicata (D1167)

Bottom Right: *Several of the regimental names could only be accommodated on double-line nameplates such as 55021* Argyll & Sutherland Highlander *although they were often incorrectly spelt in many publications, including ABCs! Much sought after by collectors, the polished brass and aluminium badge was still in place on 22nd January 1979. Such a pairing now at auction would command a strong interest and probably a very good price, as the class has its followers even in the ranks of die-hard steam enthusiasts.*
Colin Whitbread (D1168)

And Finally: *With as many as eight of the class visible on the scrap line at Doncaster Works during the Deltic Open Day on 27th February 1982, we take our last view of the Class 55s. Fortunately at least one of those in camera, 55015 (Tulyar) stood out enough to join the then growing numbers of early preserved diesels. This is a scene of potentially 26,400hp in front of us, if only it could all have been harnessed one last time from this splendid class of racehorses and regiments.*
Arthur Wilson (D1169)

We hope you have enjoyed this look back to Heritage Traction Deltics and will join us again in future volumes. However, can we offer a reminder that all of these published shots are available to purchase as superb duplicate slide copies direct from Strathwood.

The code number at the end of each slide indicates its catalogue number, and also the name of the photographer whose work we felt warranted inclusion.

To get your copy of the extensive catalogue listing of these and many thousands of other shots available in fabulous colour, please send £5.00 to: -

    Strathwood Limited
    Kirkland House
    Bruce Street, Whithorn.
    Dumfries & Galloway DG8 8PY

Or visit the websites: -
www.strathwood.com or www.railwayslide.co.uk.

In return we will send the collector's catalogue, complete with sample slide, post free to UK addresses (overseas add £2.50).